www.finishinglinepress.com

One of These Things Is Not Like the Other

To Jull,
With affection,
Your pal,
Kurt Luchs

poems by

Kurt Luchs

Finishing Line Press
Georgetown, Kentucky

One of These Things Is Not Like the Other

ACKNOWLEDGMENTS

Grateful acknowledgment is made to the following publications and their editors for
first publishing the poems collected here:

Antiphon: "Where Do We Come From? What Are We? Where Are We Going?"
Clover, a Literary Rag: "Cottonwood Seeds"
Crosswinds Poetry Journal: "The Argument," "First Flakes"
Emrys Journal: "Gray Fox"
Fjords Review: "Blizzard"
Former People Journal: "My Personal Doom," "Looking into a Face," "The Germ of an
Idea," "Focus Group"
Gander Press Review: "I Believe There Were Others"
Grey Sparrow Journal (Snow Jewel 7): "Spider"
Into the Void: "I long to enter the unholy..."
Light: "Psalm"
Minetta Review: "Homunculus"
Noctua Review: "The Sound of Weeping"
Otis Nebula: "What's-Her-Face," "Story," "Meditation"
Phantom Drift: "Natural History"
Poet's Billow: "Winter Begins" (winner of the Bermuda Triangle Poetry Prize)
Quail Bell Magazine: "Two Sisters"
Roanoke Review: "A Last Villanelle"
Sheila-Na-Gig: "Still," "Summon the Stones"
The Sun Magazine: "Mindfulness"
Triggerfish Critical Review: "Wrong Cave," "The Innocence of Youth"
Verse-Virtual: "The Dream"
Wilderness House Literary Review: "Encounter"

Publisher: Leah Maines
Editor: Christen Kincaid
Cover Art: Roberta Laine
Author Photo: Jeanine Kleman
Cover Design: Leah Huete

Printed in the USA on acid-free paper.
Order online: www.finishinglinepress.com
          also available on amazon.com

Author inquiries and mail orders:
Finishing Line Press
P. O. Box 1626
Georgetown, Kentucky 40324
U. S. A.

Table of Contents

I.

My Personal Doom 1

Still...2

Looking into a Face 3

Wrong Cave...5

What's-Her-Face 6

The Sound of Weeping...7

Natural History...8

Story 9

II.

Spider 10

Encounter 11

Two Sisters...12

Cottonwood Seeds...14

Gray Fox 15

Winter Begins 16

First Flakes...17

Blizzard 18

III.

Mindfulness..19

"Where Do We Come From? What Are We? Where Are We Going?"...20

Psalm..21

The Germ of an Idea 22

Focus Group..23

The Innocence of Youth...24

IV.

The Dream..25

"I long to enter the unholy…" 26

Homunculus..27

The Argument...28

Summon the Stones...29

I Believe There Were Others 30

A Last Villanelle..31

Meditation 32

All poetry is simply an escape from reality. It says what is palpably not true. The only difference between poets is a difference in the kind of escape they crave. Some are content with visions of a pretty girl who is also a good cook and pays for the marketing out of her own funds; others demand the insane consolations of metaphysics, or the hiding-place of a jargon no one can understand.
    —H.L. Mencken (from Minority Report, entry #28)

During one of his lecture tours of America, Dylan Thomas was asked to define poetry. He replied: "I remember once a scene in which Laurel pushes Hardy down the stairs...I can't describe it. It would have to be seen. I say this only: that it was genuine poetry in every sense."

I.

My Personal Doom

They say the universe is either made up of numbers,
information or tiny bits of energy vibrating
like mental patients receiving electroshock therapy.
Well, I wish they'd make up their minds,
the people who say those things, I mean, not
the mental patients, if indeed
there's a difference. Myself,
I'm not sure of much of anything
except the gravity that hugs me to mother earth
and keeps me from flying off into space,
incinerating in the upper atmosphere
like a shooting star in reverse,
a retroactive meteor shower.
Surely there must be some value to even
the smallest death, my personal doom
included. High above us a million such stray
celestial objects continue their clockwork walks
through the deep sky, inexorably inching
their way toward an appointed encounter
with our home world. They say
it won't be pretty, and for once
I agree with them, if only because
we won't be far enough away to objectively appreciate
the beauty of it. Aesthetics can be
so confusing when they hang on the spectral light
of billions of smoldering human souls. Sorry, I seem
to have strayed from the subject, which is
my personal doom. For the record,
her name is Roberta, and she takes the shape
of life and death, of Alpha and Omega, of stars
and those of us they fall upon,
no numbers, no information, just pure energy
and already I can feel myself beginning to vibrate
for there are worse things
than going out in a blaze of glory.

Still

There is the stillness of rot,
mold slowly, quietly overrunning and reclaiming
the fruit.
This is not that.
The stillness of fear, of children huddled in the closet
without breathing,
hiding from the drunken father.
Nor that either.
And the stillness of death, in which only the beards
and fingernails of the departed
can grow.
No.
This is something completely
other, a stillness that engenders
the more we are entangled and unable
to tell where one leaves off and the other
begins,
making sounds we can't even hear ourselves
no longer aware of ourselves,
a stillness more pronounced for being
anything but silent.
The stillness of wonder that such a moment
can still be in a world of
rot and fear and death.
When we were younger this might have led
to a baby, but that was long ago
in another life.
Still we are making something new
between us, two into one,
blue eyes and brown,
me into you,
hands cradling faces
like rivers searching for an ocean
without a shore.

Looking into a Face

Symmetrical?
Not exactly.
"There is no excellent beauty without
some strangeness in the proportion,"
said Francis Bacon,
which beats to hell anything
I could come up with.
He was probably looking in the mirror
when that line came to him
and I like to think maybe
he cut himself shaving, but I'm looking
at you,
into a face I love.
While I could happily praise your eyes, gazing into me
and beyond,
it would have to be
one at a time,
they are so different.
Meanwhile we are somewhat preoccupied
with me in you
and you under and around me and time
coming to a halt as it does
every time,
our faces so different
from each other and even from
twin parts of themselves, yet the parts
are beautiful
and the whole cannot begin to be sung.
We prefer a broken symmetry,
who knows why,
like the one they say
began the universe,
matter and antimatter annihilating each other
at ever so slightly different rates
and the tiny extra bit of matter left over
making everything that was and is and will be,
you and me,
faces and eyes,

bodies into bodies, broken
but beautiful,
world without end.

Wrong Cave

The DNA test results were conclusive: only 2.6 percent
Neanderthal. Roberta patted my head and said, "There, there," but I
was inconsolable. "Many people have as little as
1 percent," she reminded me. "And Africans have none at all."
"Yes," I said. "Then there are the lucky ones
with up to 4 percent." "Who wants to be a caveman anyway?"
she said, sitting down with her arm around my shoulder.
"We're all cavemen, just not from the same cave," I whispered
into her ear. She began to breathe faster, and whispered back,
"We're better. We're smarter. We survived." I was
kissing her savagely now, tugging a little
at her hair. "Their brains were actually
bigger," I said. "They buried their dead with wildflowers.
They made cave paintings of indescribable beauty. They must've
been more peaceful than us or they'd still be here."
Her eyes were nearly closed as she undid my top button.
"The original flower children," she said. "Personally I think
you're more than 2.6 percent." "Maybe the Neanderthals are
still here," I said. "They walk among us," she murmured,
removing her blouse. "And they vote." She pulled me on top
of her. "I doubt that very much," I sighed as I nibbled
at her breasts. "The only thing they'd do in that booth
is paint a lovely childlike picture of a woolly mammoth with
the juice from some crushed berries." She gasped,
"The people have spoken."

What's-Her-Face

They locked me in a dark room
with what's-her-face
to see which of us would emerge alive.
"Imperishable!" I hissed.
She recoiled while the word
went off to slit its wrists.
"Taxable income!" she retorted.
I was stunned, caught off guard.
I began to feel about the size of a voodoo doll.
"Total commitment!" I threw at her,
but it might as well have been a marshmallow.
"Arctic...funereal..." I was desperate
and she knew it. She paused for several years
to apply some eyeliner.
Her last words to me were: "Executive whole life."
They didn't hurt, didn't kill,
but they brought the house down
with a frail rain of sawdust.

The Sound of Weeping

The sound of weeping woke me in the night;
It was you, half-sleeping and half-awake,
Who cut the silence with a cry so white
With grief that all not broken had to break;
My heart broke with your heart, the dark dissolved
Into broken sobs caught in one white throat,
And for a moment everything devolved
On a single mournful perishing note.
Long ago I heard a loon cry, far off,
Inconsolable on the wide waters
While thunder, murmuring, stifled a cough
And rain made music in smothered gutters.
Why it wept—for what, or who—I never
Knew, though I carry that bird forever.

Natural History

I.
Today we studied the ruins.
Your eyelashes were already a legend among the Byzantines.
Once, I believed you could read the stars,
perhaps even read your own mind.
Yet you can't feel your own grave
rushing at you with its mouth open,
the branches of that place soaked in a green light,
the clenched teeth of the moon.

II.
That was some of the work I did for extra credit.

Then they made me chalk your name
a hundred times on the blackboard;
but the thought of there being so many of you,
each one the same,
each dotting her "i" with a drop of blood...
It was too much. I flinched
and hooded the blackboard with a hospital sheet.

III.
In the shorn fields
Death gathers a bouquet
of all the hands that ever touched you.

IV.
Ladies and gentlemen, my latest discovery:
the heart is a piece of coal.
Yes, a piece of coal in which the fossilized leaves
of an extinct fern
are just beginning to stir from a breeze that passed
centuries ago.
If you look closely,
at the tip of the branch is poised
an impossibly small bird, with hollow sockets that look
neither left nor right.
The bird, also, is extinct.

Story

A man is wounded by lightning.
He gets up, smoke still rising from his rags.
He takes a step, and another…
This goes on for a while.
But once touched that way,
how difficult, suddenly, to imagine
the life ahead.
What days or years could tip the scales
against such a moment?
What hand could stand the comparison?
The wound never closes;
it grows like the grin of an imbecile, and the man
sickens and dies.
The wound, however, has found a reason to live,
going about the man's business
in his shoes, in his rags.

II.

Spider

My ceiling her floor,
the very concept of ceiling absent
from her world.

She has somewhere to get to
in a hurry,
and the faster

her silent legs move
the more my heart races,
keeping time.

Such purpose
one only sees in salesmen
and murderers.

My broom a vengeful
god overshadowing
her many wide eyes.

Encounter

In the fine white gravel at my feet
something quick, alive, disturbing the dust...
It stops in my shadow—
a five-legged wolf spider.
Two legs are simply missing
while another drags brokenly behind.
We watch each other on the quiet road.
The breeze ruffles the tiny hairs on his back.
I'd like to think my soul great enough
to encompass a crippled spider
but I see nothing between us,
nothing. Half-hobbling
he's made it alone this far,
and at the approach of a curious fingertip
he's gone.

Two Sisters

Dingo is the smart one
But Wombat has the looks
In the family, a dark

Tortoiseshell with limbs
That seem cut from soft stone
And eyes deep as a green and black sea.

Age and arthritis have made her
Walk like an old Chinese woman
Carrying a bundle of sticks.

At rest though—which is twenty-three
Hours out of twenty-four—
She's the loveliest thing that ever lived.

You can't help but feel the Egyptians
Were half-right to worship them,
These creatures that own us and deign

To let us attend upon them
With our inferior offerings
Of processed fish and turkey.

We are not worthy!
Dingo has somehow divined the horrible
Secrets of the human calendar.

She knows a visit to the vet
Is nigh and hides under the bed
Howling as if her

Last kitten had been drowned.
Wombat remains ignorant and serene.
Which sister is the wiser?

To honor the feline demiurge I have
Given up reading the newspaper (no great
Loss, let's be honest)

And will devote my remaining days
To absorbing the warmth of the
One true god, the sun, that giant cat's eye.

Cottonwood Seeds

A million of them weigh less than three pounds.
No wonder they lift away on the wind,
miniature paratroopers buoyed by filaments
finer than a spider's web and carried
for miles in search of water.
The actual seed is barely visible
to the naked eye, yet each one contains
complete instructions for assembling
a tree that may reach a hundred feet
into the blue air, growing fast
though only lasting so long.
Chances are, if you planted one as a child
you have already outlived it.
But the leaves! The leaves are shining
green diamonds that shimmer in the slightest
breeze, their long stems giving them
unusual freedom of movement for prisoners.
Their rustling reminds me of a harem chamber,
the sound of silks on silks, flesh on flesh...
and now my mind is wandering
farther than any seed borne on the wind.
This image too is somehow latent
and lurking in the cottonwood seed,
worlds sleeping within worlds asleep,
tiny travelers suddenly bursting forth
by the billions to make it snow in June, in us.

Gray Fox

The scolding crows flushed him out of the brush at last.
He was about to make a break for it across Roberta's driveway,
but I waved at him and called for him to come and sit for a spell.
He cocked his head and looked at me quizzically for a moment,
then shrugged his compact fox shoulders, trotted over and sat
on his haunches right next to me. I was in a deck chair
facing the sunset, sipping a margarita. "Can I make you one?"
I said. "Thanks, I never touch the stuff," he said. I nodded.
The crows continued their caterwauling, albeit at a more
discrete distance. "The hell with the crows," I said. "Brother,
you can say that again," he said. "What is it lately anyway?
It's like the whole country has gone crazy. There's nothing but
hate, hate, hate, morning, noon and night." "What have the crows
got against you?" I said. "Beats me," he said. "It's not as if I can
climb trees to reach their nests. Hell, we don't even occupy the
same ecological niche. Do I look like a carrion eater to you?"
I had to admit that he did not. "You're one of the finest
looking creatures I've ever seen," I said. He smiled grimly.
"That and five bucks will get me a cup of gourmet coffee,"
he said. Out of nowhere I blurted, "How's the family?" He gave
me a withering look. "What family?" he said. "No fox cubs,
no Mrs. Fox?" I said. "Not anymore," he said. "I don't know
where the kids are, and the missus ran off with a red fox a
month ago." "Is that even a thing?" I said. "I mean, can two
species of fox…?" I let the words dangle in the air. "Let's just
say the lady never met a fox she didn't like," he said.
I nodded again. There didn't seem to be much more to say,
and I had no experience at consoling a fox. He too seemed
to realize the conversation was over. "Well, I'd love to stay
and chat, but I'd better be going," he said. "I have to give
those idiot crows a run for their money. So long, pal."
As he stood and trotted off I gave him a little salute. The crows
renewed their harassment and followed him deeper into
the woods, until their furious cries finally faded and blended
with the other muted sounds of twilight.

Winter Begins

Pink, gray and blue is the breath
of the sun this morning,
my own fogging the windshield
from the inside, likewise icing
the surface of my thoughts
to a pure stillness.
Twenty-three degrees and falling,
falling to who-knows-what
in the middle of God-knows-where,
a cornfield miles out of town.
I am the only mammal
moving in this landscape,
and that's only
if you count breathing.
But no, the mice must be busy too
on their underground railroad
to nowhere. Even though
I can't see them, I can feel them
gnawing at the foundation of things,
dragging stray ears of corn
into the dark earth
as they prepare
to topple an empire.

First Flakes

The day kept trying to dawn
and finally gave up, as if to say
today has been cancelled
due to lack of photons.
Nothing but wind and cold all
afternoon in the deepening gray
lashing us poor souls below.
At the hour of not quite twilight
the first flakes come down
slantwise like drunken
debutantes descending
a spiral staircase to
the bargain basement.
They giggle and collapse on
each other, beginning to pile up.
It may be months before we can
scrape away their costume jewelry.

Blizzard

This vast erasure reveals
By obscuring. Here is the
Black spine of the world laid bare
In a wash of white in which
Only the outlines persist
Of the nearest building, tree,
Telephone pole or person
Pushing against the soft, slow
Implacable tidal wave.
All reduced to archetypes,
The dim shapes loom and recede
As in a dream, leaving no
Sign that they were ever there.
And perhaps they never were.

III.

Mindfulness

I practice a very special
form of mindfulness
called not-minding-ness.
This has brought me peace and purified
my soul to the point that it is almost
possible to live with me.
My sacred principles are:
Read no newspapers.
Watch no television.
Stay the hell offline.
Do not discuss religion or politics
with anyone dumber than yourself
or smarter than yourself
for in neither instance
will there be enlightenment.
Remain silent at all costs
unless you are being tortured nonstop
in which case it is acceptable
to scream occasionally.
If a spider is crawling over you
let him crawl;
he may well be more evolved
and he comes by his poison honestly.
Above everything be still
and know that this world
means to kill us all
and will eventually succeed.
Relax. The worst has already happened.

"Where Do We Come From? What Are We? Where Are We Going?"

(Title and inscription of a painting by Paul Gauguin.)

Always the big questions
from the troubled post-Impressionists.
Well, Paul, now that you mention it,
I come from a long line of genetic mutants
whose total dysfunction is somehow
greater than the sum of its individual sadnesses.
It's a miracle any of us could master the basics
of reproduction and manage to pass on
our defective inheritance.
What I am is a piece
of dying meat that seems to think
it has time to ponder its own mortality
and the meaning—if any—of existence.
So we have that in common at least.
Where we are going is a tricky one,
seeing as there is no "we," nor am I
about to set foot in Tahiti,
and if I did, no masterpieces would emerge
because I am not an artistic genius
despite leaving my own wife behind in another world.
Still, I love your questions,
which mystify and haunt me even more
than your dark tropical canvasses.
Where are you?

Psalm

Make a joyful noise
unto the wallpaper,
let us sing unto the ice pick,
unto the man who squints
in the presence of the light.

Dear Lord, it's me!
The light is drilling a pinhole
through my head
for the angels to take aim at that pool
of grease, my life.

Someone's loving hands
pressed to my temples,
prophetic phosphenes
offering a preview
of tonight's coming attractions.

I am useless and dangerous,
or perhaps merely useless.
Why then do I wake
with blood on my fingers,
meat in the refrigerator

and a clean conscience?
From every face, in every eye
my narrow grave yawns,
bored with the prospect
of admitting me.

The Germ of an Idea

The world as we know
it is full of bacteria,
like the kind that crowds between lips
to keep the word "love" from entering or escaping,
or the kind that eats our meals
and digests them for us,
or the kind we elect to the presidency,
after which we must invent vaccines
to protect the innocent, who are also
a form of bacteria,
mostly innocuous;
even our literature,
which will soon become infested with this theme,
is written of the bacteria, by the bacteria
and for the bacteria,
who shall not perish from the earth,
as witness the gentle billions of bacilli that
have grouped themselves selflessly together
to form the letters of this
letter to them.

Focus Group

Would you like to join our focus group?
Our corporate sponsor prefers to remain anonymous,
Though you'd recognize their name if you were a blood spatter expert
With knowledge of ancient Sumerian death rituals.

They hope to learn how long a man
Can scream under water before he realizes no help is coming
And that whatever is about to devour him will soon be
Swallowed whole by something even bigger.

Would you like to take part? This prestige research project
Is sure to change the way we look at the soul
As it separates from the mortified flesh like a puffball mushroom
Exploding at midnight in the forest.

Our focus group needs you, and you, and you, if only
Because the digging will go so much faster, and the placing of stones,
And the numbering of atrocities will add up to so much more
Than the square root of a charred and paralytic zero.

The Innocence of Youth

They all come to me, even the crazies. Especially the crazies.
The nice young couple were nearly out of their minds
with worry, and no wonder. For three nights running,
paintings of the most disturbing scenes imaginable had
appeared directly over their baby's crib, scrawled on the ceiling
by the hand of some sadistic human prankster. "Or
maybe a poltergeist," the wife suggested. I suppressed
a chuckle and examined the pictures on her cell phone.
The grin died on my face, stillborn. These paintings were beyond
horrifying. They made Heironymous Bosch look like
Norman Rockwell. Severed body parts, mutant monstrosities,
elaborate torture machines, smoke, lightning, lava, blood and
broken glass everywhere. Every morning the husband
whitewashed the ceiling and every night there somehow
appeared another scene of utter desolation and depravity
in its place. "Anything on the nanny cam?" I said. "Nothing
but static," said the wife. And when they tried to stay awake
to catch the perpetrator, exhaustion had defeated them.
"I'll take the case," I said. That night I camped by the crib
with a cup of coffee, a flashlight and a copy of *Confessions
of an English Opium Eater*. Just after 1:30 a.m. there
was a rustling in the crib and a dim golden glow. I turned my
eyes from De Quincey in time to see the infant levitating
slowly toward the ceiling, emanating a visible aura like the baby
Jesus, with a palette in one hand, a brush in the other, and an
adorable black beret tilted on his tiny bald head. I shined
the flashlight on him and he didn't even blink, he was
totally absorbed in his work. So was I. As he dabbed
his brush here and there, touching up his masterpiece,
the painting began to make sense to me. It was dark and
agonizing, sure, but there were bits of hope and light as well,
a dog that was not on fire, a lidless eyeball with a somewhat
cheerful gleam. I turned off the flashlight and tiptoed away,
resolved to tell the parents nothing. Let's face it, the tyke
had talent. He was practically a miniature Picasso. I wanted
to see his Blue Period.

IV.

The Dream

Five years old, I dream
of the dark and a terrible dance.
Amid gravel and driven dust
squats a town of wretched little pueblos,
no more than walls, really, open to the sky.
There the townspeople move as one, spasmodic,
soundless in their circling.
As my eyes grow accustomed to the night
I see they are joined in a crooked line
by a length of crooked
pipe welded to their heads.
I'm afraid; I run; they follow and catch me.
They fuse me to the pipe and I stop struggling.
Suddenly I'm one of them;
I can appreciate their point of view.
I see they are beautiful
and the dance meaningful.

"I long to enter the unholy…"

I long to enter the unholy
veins of lightning
like the sound of breaking glass,
to trace the shudder that
flashes through clouds and shakes
the dead in their new shoes;
to lie down in the soft coffins of long grass
as in a woman's thighs,
and never breathe again
unless my breathing were the wind.

I long to fall forever
between stars, into the dark
like a hole someone is still digging;
to burrow in the drifts of snow like silence;
to be the shadow that walks away
when a man dies.

Homunculus

Oracle or pincushion, which did they intend
who fashioned him from a single reed
and a whitening lock of human hair?

The mouth a vicious daub of red,
partially healed and not meant
for speech.

The ears still green;
buds, perhaps, opening for a syllable
yet to be named,

a hissing song. Whatever it is
the tiny fists have closed on,
they aren't letting go.

The feet mere stubs fit not even for planting.
At his side the painted blade hangs blue and ready.
What color the eyes, rolled inward forever?

The Argument

Impossible?

When the moon tells stories
and the olive trees believe them,
huddled, their leaves quivering.

When the wind limps from roof to roof
and tries on, briefly, a paper hat, tilted
in the green light.

Impossible?

When the feather in the paperweight
shivers, struggles to rise,
edges toward the glass…

When the shoes, now a little out of style,
feel an urge for the sea,
for the endless stairs of water.

Impossible. Or maybe—

when your eyes tell me,
and your precise hands, folded that way—
impossible!

Until the memory of things once possible
is like a candle we burn for someone
buried alive.

Summon the Stones

Summon the stones,
we'll hold them accountable,
we'll make them answer
held at gunpoint for seven years.
I would speak
with them for news
of the planet.
I'm anxious to hear
the gossip of the dust,
I understand
the quartz does not include me
in its white dreams,
the sands
in low tones are passing
a name
one to the other.
Not our name.
And they say
the mountains have joined hands,
building paradise
behind our backs
while we stare at the widening
crater before us,
speechless,
turning to stone.

I Believe There Were Others

To keep myself awake I keep telling myself the old story
of how I woke up in the room. Of course I don't know how
I got here. Of course that doesn't concern me. Naturally
the door is locked. That concerns me, but what can I do?
I've screamed myself blue through the cracks to no end,
not even a breeze in return. For all I know it's a closet
and I've been pleading with some dead man's underwear.
From what I can tell the air on the other side—if there is one—
smells like the air in here: like walnuts. No, I haven't
found any walnuts. No, I don't have amnesia. I know who I am.
There's a mirror on the door for reminding myself, although
the man in the glass looks every bit as mystified.
I've pulled the lint from my pockets and run my fingers
over the pores of stale paint on the walls that stare me down.
I found a dead orb weaver hugging itself in a corner.
Yes, there's a clock. Yes, it's stopped. It's been a quarter
to nine for years. At times I feel sure I'm not the first.
I'm positive I've seen someone else's footprints in the
gathering dust where I pace for miles before I realize
I'm following myself. I know things are happening
at the corner of my eye. When I turn around suddenly
to see if everything's the same, it always is, but in my heart
another tree topples and I find it that much harder to believe
in four yellow walls and a light bulb. I believe there were
others. I believe they emptied the medicine cabinet and left
a deck for solitaire with the one-eyed jacks asleep. Also half
a pack of cigarettes, but I don't smoke. I'm thinking of
starting though.

A Last Villanelle

To Brett Foster, 1973-2015

The best beauty is of things as they go.
I sing the fading sigh, the falling leaf.
Beauty passes, and passing makes it so.

I celebrate the loss of all I know,
The sure opinion and unsure belief.
The best beauty is of things as they go.

I watch things die where some would watch them grow.
Glory comes with whatever comes to grief.
Beauty passes, and passing makes it so.

So much better the arrow than the bow,
And better the mad flight, however brief.
The best beauty is of things as they go.

No sight compares with the sun sinking low,
Turning waves gold as they break on the reef.
Beauty passes, and passing makes it so.

I seek the final fire, the final snow.
Finality itself is my motif.
The best beauty is of things as they go.
Beauty passes, and passing makes it so.

Meditation

The long shuddering intake of breath
From the air conditioner
Plays its one plaintive note
For all it's worth
So much feeling in that undying
Death rattle
I believe more than the air
Is being conditioned
And behind it the cry of crickets
Where there are no crickets
The crickets are in me
All of this is somewhere in me
And I am somewhere else
A vista opening upon a verge
Scenes waiting to become sounds
Sounds waiting to become words
Words waiting to become thoughts
Thoughts waiting to remake the world
Because the world they behold
Is unbearably bright and utterly silent
Strange and beautiful and terrifying

Kurt Luchs has written all of his life for nearly every medium. He began as a poet, and has published poems, plays and literary essays in such publications as *Former People Journal, Into the Void, Minetta Review, Poydras Review, Triggerfish Critical Review, Otis Nebula, Sheila-Na-Gig, Right Hand Pointing, Roanoke Review, Wilderness House Literary Review, Crosswinds Poetry Journal, Grey Sparrow Journal, Noctua Review, Quail Bell Magazine, Antiphon, Light, Phantom Drift, Fjords Review, Verse-Virtual, The Ibis Head Review, Burningword Literary Journal, The Poet's Billow,* and *Emrys Journal, The Sun Magazine, Clover, The Charles Carter* and *Bramble,* among others. As a humorist he has contributed to such prominent outlets as the *Onion,* the *New Yorker* and *McSweeney's Internet Tendency.* His work has been represented in most of the Onion books, including *Our Dumb Century,* winner of the Thurber Prize for humor, and in a number of anthologies, including *May Contain Nuts* (HarperCollins), *Created in Darkness by Troubled Americans* (Knopf/Random House) and *Moms Are Nuts* (Vansant Creations). Barnes and Noble published his book *Leave the Gun, Take the Cannoli: A Wiseguy's Guide to the Workplace,* a collection of gangster movie quotes and commentary applied to best practices. In television, he has written comedy for Bill Maher at *Politically Incorrect* and Craig Kilborn at the *Late Late Show.* In radio, he was a staff writer for the comedy prep service the Complete Sheet, and later for American Comedy Network, which he also managed. Since 2002 he has edited and frequently contributed to *The Big Jewel,* a leading site for literary humor, which he co-founded. In 2017 Sagging Meniscus Press published his humor collection, *It's Funny Until Someone Loses an Eye (Then It's Really Funny).* He is currently writing an autobiographical novel with the working title of *Honey Street,* under the theory that because it's a novel, no one will be able to sue him. He lives in Kalamazoo, Michigan, where he manages a group of radio stations and a top-secret government experiment known only as the Inhuman Genome Project.

CPSIA information can be obtained
at www.ICGtesting.com
Printed in the USA
BVHW042350200319
543288BV00005B/23/P

9 781635 348750